KNOT

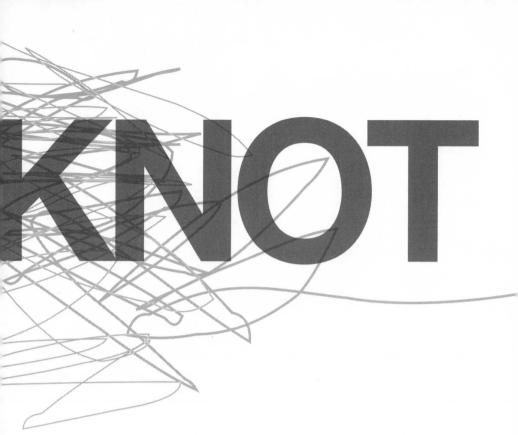

POETRY BY STACY DORIS

The University of Georgia Press   Athens and London

Published by The University of Georgia Press

Athens, Georgia 30602

© 2006 by Stacy Doris

Set in Helvetica Neue

Printed and bound by McNaughton and Gunn, Inc.

The paper in this book meets the guidelines for
permanence and durability of the Committee on
Production Guidelines for Book Longevity of the
Council on Library Resources.

Printed in the United States of America

10   09   08   07   06   P   5   4   3   2   1

Library of Congress Cataloging-in-Publication Data

Doris, Stacy.

Knot : poetry / by Stacy Doris.

p. cm. — (Contemporary poetry series)

ISBN-13: 978-0-8203-2813-3 (pbk. : alk. paper)

ISBN-10: 0-8203-2813-8 (pbk. : alk. paper)

I. Title. II. Contemporary poetry series (University of Georgia Press)

PS3554.O6728K58 2006

811'.54—dc22   2005025240

British Library Cataloging-in-Publication Data available

"What would it mean to remain faithful to what is never present? What would it mean to represent what is always passing before us? What happens when our eyes meet what they cannot see, when they encounter what cannot be encountered? What would an iconography of evanescence look like? Is it possible to perceive a process of vanishing? In what way is sight essentially linked to an experience of mourning, an experience that mourns not only our vanishing experience but sight itself?"

"Vanishing Remains," Eduardo Cadava

Acknowledgments

Thanks to the editors of the following publications in which excerpts of *Knot* have appeared:

Review of Two Worlds, *War and Peace*, *Parthenon West*, *Small Town*, *Antennae*, *Commonweal*, *Bay Poetics*, *Dirty*, *1913: A Journal of Forms*, *Fourteen Hills*, and *New American Writing*. *Le temps est à chacun* (Marseille: Contrat Main) is a version of «iii.IV» rendered in French by Martin Richet.

I am grateful to Chet Wiener, Sarah Riggs, Cole Swensen, Lisa Robertson, Martin Richet, Charles Alexander and Robert Kocik for their critical readings of this material in its various stages. Thanks too to Kurt Ozment for his help.

This book is dedicated to the living: in particular Sarah, Omar, and Inky. It is also dedicated to the unborn.

Contents

Entrance

A New Life   o

Under Fire   i.I – i.XIX

Bottleneck, being a limbus   ii.I – ii.XIX

Pair (Parity)   iii.I – iii.XIX

KNOT

Entrance

What follows occurs in a moment; a flash. It would detail a single tangibility if that did not entail all sensation. So it tries. Its impossible ambition is a critique of everything that isn't anarchy. The proto-characters, mock-canto structures and Dantean echoes, being apocryphal—a sort of integral postscript—stem from indistinctions between inner and exterior, so I let them. Similarly, the deformed or queered pronouns and the myriad disagreements between nouns and verbs reflect the need to reexamine imposed disjunctions among singulars and plurality. I could not find a more elegant way to pursue this inquiry, and chose not to silence it nevertheless.

Form means we keep changing our minds, at every velocity, due to life; poetry is that fact's lucidity. This book's actual shape is a meander that articulates its construct by showing all of its vantages at once, including the movement which creates them. Each path encodes the evidence that light or clarity is flawed, and proceeds relationally. Or, the thread is the way words lead, at their best, to betrayals in all domains (epistemology and the other -ologies, the social sciences, metaphysics and the quotidian) while remaining indentured to the hoax of inquiry itself. Everywhere tethered, language is the vehicle of all our discoveries, each one myopic. And in its interplay lies our hope.

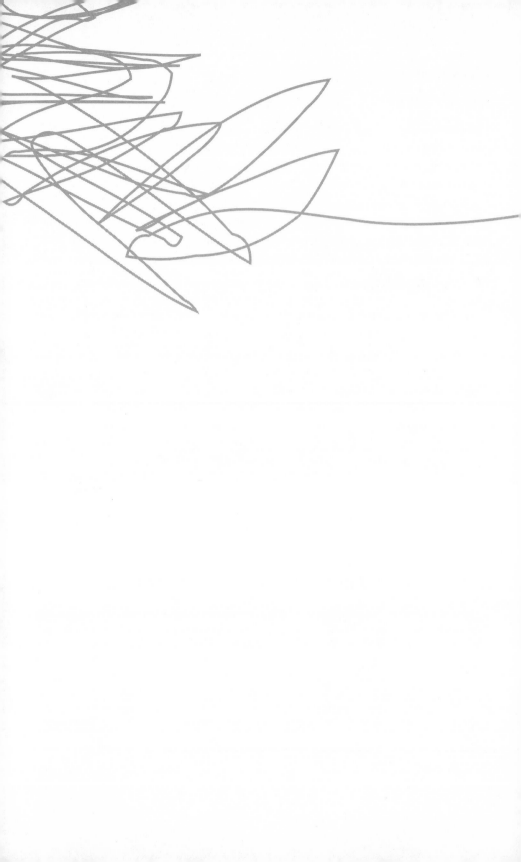

A New Life

Inconceivable. Wrought as a monument, forgery thus, everywhere
Crystallized to carbon and tinkering. Many throats silted or blocked

From breath. Purely so, with inadmissible drunkenness, each follicle
Soaked poisons so radiantly laced, they mixed with touch, became

Guilt for part of demise's richness; a ridicule of judgment. For us, a
Lot ended.

Under Fire

Are collisions entrances? Even if inhuman, can't they merit collapse,
Without ingress, seeding, or proper nourishment? Detonations, no order,
Range increasingly discrete with the tear of—was it a garment? If we aren't
Propelling ourself, was somebody? With magnets? A kiss? Whatever's
Small and round, a purchase.

"Tick, tick," says the cat. "Tick." Here's a present. Here's a collection,
The real Halloween. Here's a gift, an igloo, so incubate, now. Something
With its eyes sealed inspects obscurity. If the lids burst: luminousness.
Here's a flowering, top-secret, then. In imagination it's hard, to invade,
And elsewhere easy or soft. A disappointment. Is this electric? With a

Switch? You shows up where somebody makes you's. Otherwise curtaining,
Present of red. Anyone comes and colors in another, filled, replaced. Unless
A burning, slight, an itch, all along the knuckles, expand, unconcerned.
Pinching continues until my's cover—was it a dress, milk?—becomes scrim.
A screen's demise, where sifting files texture's collapse, through noticing.
To see is not credulity, just dissolution.

Into some distance, everything empties. Explosions riddle nightfalls now,
And bombs partly originate sound; thus echo unending. In radiance, cells
Determine clashes and covering. Convert. Somebody, numb, sheathes in
Incomprehension. But touch medicates. In each caress, we takes shape as
Dwelling's axis. So another's hand insulates us, cocoons meaning cordons.

"Harmony" and "form," each song, these constructs serve law. So in a
Realm independent of time, there's disequilibrium's chance. In accepting
Erosion, embracing drowning, anyone could indefinitely swim. In giving up
You's a permanence, soaked rather than encircled, confusion of saturate
With restore, in lost recourse to fixing. Reparation's repartition, a sharing
For those who won't recognize others, so invent them as subservience.
Then living forever predicates eruption. Repatriation. The bullets stands
For blessings, so freedom's enduring.

Exposure's a safety. Stripped to the invisible. Security heats what it protects
Into bursting. Attracts to the lasting cover of ash. Any benison targets
Believers. Marks or wounds them thus, as winding too cuts off.

Impulse, meaning light, may blind, thus spare anyone from balance; from
Justice. Radiance might impose equilibrium, but dazzling's uncertain;
Luminous is dangerous. Thus a hug darkens, womb means shadow and such.
Cloaking, due process can't pierce, only engulf. Consumes without chewing
Or digestion. Breath constitutes alignment; triggers every muscle, voluntary
Or not, in sleep and full attack, and unravels motion's force into toxins,
Meaning aftermath. Hunger poisons biochemically, wreaks war on its own
Borders. Swallowing or being swallowed whole doesn't change that.

In the choice between failure and change, loss becomes most appealing.
Defeat has its strength, while alteration legislates weakness. In claiming
Flexibility, a system's irregular, unstable thus. Admits death. Detonation
Invokes protection by deactivating vitality. In an explosion, all things are
Created equal, in the eyes of dissolution. Thinking wears down, derails any
Thought in progress. Then though understanding's no option, everyone
Refuses permeation, opts to end instead, to lose rather than open.

Any life's an example of living, thus lacking substance, an in-between,
Commanded. Where patches stand for bodies. Each day's contained
By the needs it fulfills, in ignoring urges, thus finite, kaput. Disbanded from
Sequence, time can't enforce habit. Bombardment rips it from conclusion,
Strings hours to gaping, to such mouths as never close. If we can eat
Everything, nothing's outside, and we'll go on. If there's nothing to eat,
We've starved out the world and it's ours to determine.

Their meeting reduced to one vibrant thread—a long stretch of sand—
Details perhaps what anyone fashions in waiting. Only with a desert
There's no end, and the occasion's all decrease, barnacled as in turned
Opposite—unsucking, as a wish to be known means, paradoxically,
Reaching instead. Then comes the cat, crying "integrate death,"
As if that were a captive or in need of a visa. Why a ship, or any mirage,
And nature, feel bankrupt inside. So that if skin's a grid, lineament's
Matted. Any darkness goes only so far, to its horizon, then turn back.
Such is called "mystery" or "miracle" or "mirror" or "marriage," all in one.

Cell says cluster and there are only two here, despite what's unfinished.
If the net of every layer articulated rather than packed, porous so
Transparent, they could get close. Approach. In nature which is built,
Plants constructed or contract to read through each other, deep,
In insufficient folds. Start with twigs. Once a tree's gone it thus instantly
Fills in. So there's no disappearance, except for the flashes of objects.
And air define replacement. Since even a cocoon's exactly located, entirely
Consumes its spot, each activity separates, wrapping us. I trails a rationale
Of foods, lovingly intentioned, so that absorption preempts sorting.
So breath balloons without moisture's extension. To chew bleeds, though
Any strand's a series of undulance, a rocking.

Did we's slip in some kind of arena, plan of a trap door or outskirts,
Roughest so it must be a center, inspecting? Sound, regardless of hearing,
Trample our organs. The part of anyone that won't stop is infectious.
We're highways then, and rawhide, in a distant stretched warming. An
Immense school vacation, this converts light to sugar, nutritional so deaf,
But nothing buds; a code's not introduced. Somebody twists acts as if
They're a unity, evidence of digesting. Clings to this engulfment; hope-
Ridden. Optimist. Then home is this thing in the ground, which caves in.

Mortality operates relative to humans. Plants, animals and others
Extinguish to what continues: dust, air, recombination. Anyone's death
Is a beforehand of varying lengths, but our living ends only for some other
People. You's can't quit yourself, are thus ongoing in your own terms, and
Corpses occur in dwelling over finitude; premonitions of how organs
And their senses will leave utterly off.

Even where time engulfs such an omission; limps on, punctured,
No consensus arises. Taboo, thus. But what's articulate in one place
Becomes decorative with exportation, a motif or wandering. Applied, so
Silent. Some habit, an existence, can then freeze in mid-stride, lose
Consistency. Shock. Where an excess of components, any plethora,
Displaces, which is called incorporeal, from extraction. Invoked, a cell's
Exceeded, in confusion, thus disorganized, implodes.

Bombardment claims retracing's unlike recall, so a conjectured path; time's
Shape, disguised as a compendium, lexical, implies potential stems from
Deformations. Aberrance squelches homogeneity, so blocks proceeding's
Way. Monster is a series of priorities attacking in specks, clamorous, the
Sound from without, unabated to depicting; enhanced beyond organic, rife
With its own contradictions, so present. Then rage's ease, adjacent, and
Breathing's external, thus trembles. Freak, as in respiration, surges only
Where nothing's steady. "Life" from "burst."

i.V

All anyone wanted was to be alive. More alive. But with the unappealing
In suspension, the enrobing, the farce, where I becomes shrine. Is explosion
Part of how to hold, there's no contact but rather the tip of what's
Palpable, breath as preparation, which should calm or quiet, but pains, so
That the edge, no longer bearing, splits? "This most peripheral trail, there's
Your path," says the cat, as if we's umbilical. In the light of circulation,
Anyone looks for payment, to grace or gain.

Where they meet, known as an entry, that's disappearance in the shape of
Constellation. To eat's perhaps the one practice for this strangeness,
Breaking bread, through its tunneling and hives, dense cells, where satiety,
If recognized, is sacrament, where digestion renders fiber's walls
Transparent, if fleeting, where, if in flashes, movements coordinate. My's
Mouth confuses almonds with cavities, swallow with keeps, friction and
Subsist. Removing from ourselfs by the fact of respiration, so oxygen grip
Departure, anyone's every span's a collapse. Enjoy as termites do, sucking
Out the marrow with a straw, drilling through nerves to numbness. Where
Air balls. Where leaves advance, a tightrope.

"Couple is representation," says the cat. "Skin exposing then covering
Constitutes a wound." This is how a pair of bodies can gouge love's
Singularity. And everyone still chews. Technique, an exercise of hours via
Days, is apt because of death, which artifice conducts. To scrape back to
Touch so that motion span waiting, activity must be inactive like growth,
Accrue from reversals, outside-in. Answer what frays the thread between
Profusion and joy, such that you has neither? So that freedom thrusts
Upon us, more than muzzling, a long punch?

i.VI

Every acceptance may recognize an end, permit outcomes thus, but skillful
Uncovering has strength to negate, and nobody can act without art.
In expression, facts lock into yes and no, an alternance. Words are then
Positive while insubstantial. Promise. So vocabulary's each culmination's
Vehicle, even in dance, lexical, meaning limited. Meaning joy, celebrated
In finitude's context, assume a greater span upon ending. Since what's
Mortal's fettered, fulfillment extols death.

Each moment, fifteen pounds of air pin us by gravity. Then anyone
Needs sixteen pounds of lightness to ever budge. Such compliance
Demands levitation, must generate excitement, which passion enact;
Thus dreams have all they can handle. From a stone, anchored, is how
We rise, where faith is placed only in potential, miracle without
Dimension's measure so opening, unhinged at least, where each "they"
Is porous, in penetrability dunked and enriched.

"In the explosion," says the cat, "the whole world becomes a skin,"
Meaning ash coated every ledge and cranny, for good. Production then
Strung on dismantlement, an augmenting transparence where, seen as a
Model, renovation's inconceivable.

Explosions stock increments, running fingers through, fantasy of recall
So that contact accrue, building, between summits, an improved dizziness.
Could disease support or result from that? Is infection to dive, spring away
From surfaces, firstly skin, to undercut blood and bone in a rush for heart
And spine where focus entails decay, which climax barters consciousness;
Where, turning back, any regard vanish? Somebody's wound is a forest, at
Least burgeons, with a rash's sense of competition. This soothes us.

Dissolution threads a skein, the slow rub of one against the other called
Recovery. It burns. No hole, because passage is imperfect. To leave is to sew
A strand of withdrawals. To nest. Breath may descend, a thrust, suspect.
Would trestle and decorate if what's described are not necessarily dead.
Others makes you's more and less human. Others and needles. Or wealth,
Which punctures most finely, surrounds those who know it, yet soporific.
A dollar's a string. So's any bill. "You're a cadaver," hums the cat. "No
Need to count."

To thirst is a corpse; a horizon is. Inability, when there's no reach, nurses
Fatigue, in the way of food, since awareness mimics ignorance but sensed.
Otherwise, passion recounts expenditure, transports, perpetuation of
Helplessness, its value. Or, response means indirect. So acquisition's
Designed to repeal panic. Humanity insists there should be no end to that.
Refuge is to take in, a downfall, and anyone hesitates, then cede. Where
Populous flowers squelch others, as blooming is bellicose, we's know
Profusion stems putrid, but hope, watching growth and ruin in one spot,
Thin layers, as pounding on aches sometimes works.

i.VIII

Whatever's white may be a maggot. Pale flies, expired, articulate sloughing
Where foliage corrodes: in and from any air, to and fro, busily. Market.
Vermin burrow, fist into all tissue, proliferate thus. Music is cellular,
Called piercing, so passage flinch or part, in a wrap considered open.
Instrument says "operate," "agree," or "at once." Upon: trumpet.

Bruise pools: a holiday for blood, where water's a roundness masked
As a circus. A ride. Where the eggs is: spring. Mass says nourishment
So incandescence counts, fungal, frank or blunt. Spreads by bleaching,
Contagiously ignites. Drunk on air, which is prayers, furling and then
Blind, believers stand as candles, expressing decimation to illustrate
Endless. Their voices, the wings burned off, worm, so creeping soars.
Contemplation's a poultice, leaches transient except in cadavers, when it
Slows, and warmth infuses since light still serve growth. Also routes,
But not in a regular way. Somebody, if a corpse, melts: a reflection of love;
Stain on time.

Pain externalize, so there's offspring, says medicine. Scars bridge when
Anyone turns, thus a fairgrounds. Carted off then, we're some souvenir,
Remembered, so invisible, eked out, so a living. In a carcass, every point
Makes sense, palimpsest, tends to glass, replete. Even if opaque, corrodes,
Thus grows. Oxidizing blossoms, so spring means carrion. Then there's no
Sorting us from verdant. Bursting, to heal are to flower inversely. To mourn
Is also sunshine; an incision.

Where action doesn't exist, meaning in life, can they cover or recast us? In
Bereavement. Gathering comes to thank death, as does love, partly since
The notion of unending closeness can't be based in any live form, except
For points, aspects, exchanges, where most of the material's petrified.
Contingent on noticing, since ultimate awareness may be exclusive
Observance of decay.

Everywhere burning once was, thus all earth's air, is still on fire. People
Start in ignition; continue, self-consuming. Walking's conflagration, a surge
Of flames that run among corners. Thus all bodies propel. We's are carved
In the trajectory of organs; further undone by joining. To collect, as dusk
Or dust, is an aside, since consumption holds what never quits, shuts out
Replacement, thus not an issue of defeat. Disappearance makes way for
Words and explanations: loss is any voice's path. Dwells on what's gone,
Chewing it not with the wash of extinction, an object's privilege, but rather
Whole, therefore in pieces, geared to realignment.

To act, voluntarily or not, is to stray; unfaithful. To respond is give up,
So a loss. Misery holds the assembled; fasten or fosters need into praise.
Where words are corporeal, to soothe or prick, diverted. Drunkenness
Replaces the drone of oscillation, and, with declaiming, celebrates, among
Peers, because the collection must be god. So hurting's being's supreme,
Which shatters through, in speech. That is compassion; to gulp down.

Hunger's some link to achieving, a root into any day, coastal. Only rice
Brings fulfillment. Only granules, comfortably sticking, hot, unconcerned
Or oblivious. If death were such a grain, and it is, why shouldn't everyone
Accept its loop? Why fight this clumping up's richness? So we don't, says
The cat, so does. To live somewhere means fit for a vacuum cleaner. Place
Then impossible in terms of specifics. An apartment: vertigo. Upstairs so
Dusk. In a room, seated, to see is to spy and soreness finds an odor: lilac.
Thus bruises stir. Rice, white, by contrast undecorative, burrows, worm
Or parasite, knuckling. It winds, the same as what a story's worth.

A speck of rice in fact defies its end, starting from dry and scratch, pumped
In saturation to a glistening unity, foments attachments. In digestion, a rice
Grain glories: fans to perhaps fingernail stature, coaxes and soothes the
Tract's linings themselves, augments all functions. Aging, where even this
System will disband, requires, to succeed, the most attentive rerouting of
Fibers so that feeling's more raw, wired to combustion's constant edge.
Because decay means danger, treachery's depth. A first step would be
Grinding teeth, all the nerves in your mouth whittled, unhidden by
Enamel, a grin.

Why is seeing reading, all technology, coded and lateral or not, an identity?
Recognition through condensing everything to symbols, including what's
Invisible. Such perception obscures all there is behind its optics. The world's
Protected then, or merely unplugged, counts down. So "clean" is the basis
Of any linearity, thus order, and age a rebellion of filth, of twisted options;
Tardy, resistant emptying, crafty recombination, pared paring, suspect,
Thus deforms, unlegitimized. Where shape's example's the starch again,
Bloated past placement, thus maturing's comic, a compromise struck, and
Movement's adjustment.

If there's ever identification, that's longing. It mopes, tree-like, rooted yet
Disconsolate. Are birds some of minutes' pockets, or is it natural, this
Bobbing, where leaves release, catching in ignition, thus "spring"? If acts
Graft, each can function as a branch added, permanent in terms of living,
But not. One at most coats or peppers the next, dropping hints, circles,
A figuration. Lets go: dizzy voltage. Where sight recycles, we's glue back in
Place differently, artificial as ever.

In retreat, they're a coil, spark that implodes, will never perhaps open.
The green sucking down into leaves, we jealously sense without touching.
Such concentration inebriates us, even without objects. Consistently
Unspoken, venerating may result in a self, unfocused and blotchy, yet it
Spreads. Then wrap holds belief. Once bandage needs no wounding or
Perhaps the hurt is impulse, one that shies away, harm marks, and you's
Afford no prevention. Somebody turns more numenal, clouded, to envelop
With an improvement on limbs. But where love surges from and is paralyzed
By need, meaning in perhaps every case, does its deformity twist?

"This is one good thing about time, how there's no need for it," says the cat,
Definitive and formless, so American perhaps. Growth, a kind of prayer,
Contradicts hours in a show of dispersal, where what's to be closed in on,
Isolated, is blood, meaning everything invisible, all that composes water,
Each duct. Again, sound. Anyone, in adoration, might wish the air different
As a present to somebody, gentler scarf never pictured or required, a
Mounting so stairs is useless, so the river lifts, so an alarm or all ringing
Trace the most delicate attention, and the atmosphere more clearly folds,
Where privacy's a gift of skin: marking.

i.XII

Money's from repeatedly asking, which disgusts. So's companionship
Perhaps. To live in iteration or any moment's stream paralyzes and
Silences, where civilized is counting's prime return. Where to pick at
Or worry a fiber, even in conformity or pattern, spoils texture. And phrases
Don't complete because alphabets forge paths; underground corridors.
Where is ambers, which reputedly captures or preserves? In air, so all in all,
There aren't ends to any step's echoes; no bridge back to the bland fizz
Of ice milk, depilatory scents, nodes labeled "home," a voice. Recycling's
That uninflected.

Love says give up and touch immolates. If not, a middle drowns, absent,
Mere, confused, while clarity pledges; threatens on an edge. But "brim,"
As any instrument, body in the abstract, ruminates meaning dreams
Functionally, proceeds by elimination, cut backs, and vacations, sporadic.
The lake, subject to freezing, shows focus but by forgery, not even pools,
Not even tips, not budging. Eats due to abundance; hungers otherwise.
Seethes, the pond. Then a part sets off, a tick, unhinged in the span
Between useless contributions. Chrysanthemums or any feathered bloom,
A draught.

Configurations hollow apprehending by increment, by repetition, which
Overturns momentum, so leaves and ropes pattern and tell no chain; defer
Seasons, flatten days to an option. So disease can detach a route. So cellular
Equal binge or, obversely, gaping. Healing and illness are communal,
Group, stick and fault to every member, swallows. Looming or seeded from
A book or glance, how else could sound make it from one place to the next
As a unit? Except that particles conspire, lodged in each wave, in
Overwhelming homogeneity, so bound. As if all air's wasabi, only mild,
Where stinging's missed.

From metabolism, we're now eating what we's swallowed yesterday or the
Day before even. Anyone lives in the past, thus, if physically. Absorption is
Rare, and catapults quick to any future. Tomorrows, existent when time's
Unknown, make, since tenuous, good subjects for somebody's faint kind of
Presence. Suspension's the sustenance of retaining's habits, unable to last
Or go on, thus still alive, held in the groove of one breath, rocking balance.

What you're synthesizing, from two days ago's snack, may be a type of fat
Lyonnaise salami baked whole into thick milky bread, which has a name
That everybody ignores, and is most certainly an element of regional pride.
I assimilates a source of national distinction or identity, anterior by all
Accounts, without knowing what to call it. Is whatever gets inside thus lost
To tracking? Can we be present in strands, in the guts, which is all we are?

Living somewhere silences, though organs must be noisy, just your's
Alertness to their sounds is marginal. Location's a periphery of digestion,
Variable, narrowly accounted. That might engage, could divvy what little
Sensation, but instead of watching we's wait, so frame somebody's arrival
With warmth, indefinite suspense. Which becomes practice, is a tale, retold,
Bursts. What breaks showers, gives liquids, provides.

i.XIV

A city, its center, where miles coil in, are darkness, and anyone living
Here goes blind, starting with color: bold punches, its opacities competing.
The midst distills, thick yet ambered, so we's are alcoholic, boyish, choke
Where hues are so creased that's what's inhaled. Exactly focused, urban,
Pigment fends vision, protects its dried liquid thus, helium. There, sight
Ricochets, so destination disorients. Since cecity forces and inflicts and
Fakes out and exacts faith, where the sky cave in comes illumination.

In atmosphere, any product's poison. It thickens the air to dimmed
Particles where breath itself's a spritz, a headache, and we're asthmatic.
Toxins and pains bog in drowsing. Dreams may be drizzle then, valorized.
What's dead yet still moving flares up, vaporizing what's touched. Thus
Vampire's brightness but the core is not that, rather a vigilance so
Unremitting it sink low-grade, fogs, mystic, spinning reduced to a hiss,
Pipe, where to witness drains, where a hand makes all inquiries, so groping,
But exposed as if to beg, sees and turn stony from waiting, rewarded thus
A pillar, stuck, angry and passive. Take him.

A day in which two hairs were removed, and that's all, and not at the same
Time: perfection. The roots still exist, but independent. Deferral always
Dazzles. Is good as an effacement, yet persists. Then I goes, pinched
And burning, sustained by the utmost faintness of attention, cramps; net of
Slippage, wrenched by garlic, out and on so installed. Where we's aren't
A casualty is chemically off; aberrant. Somebody's romance, in a city's
Middle, is stasis, what lenses mask, love as black and white, a trail. Not
There so secure. Absent so to worship. Object so subject to hugs and lavish
Girls; a slave, where civic equals exile yet expels, circles, so retinal: iris or
Filter so clouding, glass so effacing, so memory. Frittering, the place grows
In and on fears.

It fires. Files and fills where we're circuitry, so utterly burned; young.
Thus urban glorifies to crackling. A city, meant as where consciousness
Conserves, based on a compromise, now reduce memory to movement,
When success is in charting, a trajectory, making way, thus wealth. Here,
Judgment's molecular, encoded so rejected. Stained. Flooding thus afloat.
In the thing we're all a part of: nothing or netting, so progressive's
Increasingly participation, so offspring: everyone's bearings herald
Blindness. Urbanity also is prejudice or love, unseeing. The leaders
Set out to locate what they've pictured, with blinkers, thus guilty, heroic.

Here, repetition incites until it ceases. We's play out its minimum
Requirements. Each application coats with some sheen, just as all painting,
Any sense of brush, corrodes. Once in the stream of action you's vanish
In our same midst. Branches redirect breath, so to continue quickly turns
Respiration unnatural. Then to inhale can envelop; umbrella. Discernment
Circles, a waiting that weighs, a prurience, to peel; remorse or remove
Where measure bog down; obscures. They behave, so tailor apprehension
To a politics; swaps existence for iteration.

To clean is a confession. Is all removal archaeology then? And rumination
Scratches. Takes grass as an appliance. Fixes it. When what's uncovered
Is empty, recognition's success. Organs store, thus an impression of abundance,
And everything else takes stock. Bodies are products but in ignorance,
Thinking to act differently, separate, deleted. Even as dust could they mix?
Particles act out adjacencies; impose. What grows sifts and absorbs, recycles,
Trades from the first, dishonorably saturates. There are charts. Exchange
Aims to carry plus consume, where how each accepts indicts all others,
So that possible enjoyment's an offer of blindness, proposition to vacate,
Though laden. Then accident welcomes. Because roads come with directions.

i.XVI

Talk eliminates imagined moments, in a rhyming of years. Certain
Birdsongs function as its web, thus denature, tonally mount where words
Decorate phrasing, hung on a tune's line, flap in the sense of breezes alone.
Babies take wing in speech then, into the blue of logic's arabesques.
Recounting threads in a row, inches, replies meaning pleats. The vocal
Twist, a chord, inflects so stamp, marks an occasion as a blight on time's
Strings, aberrant, a standstill. Mirrored or lined by meaning, to speak
Devours or decimate instants; mocks and haunts any event to illusion.
Conflict reforms to a mirage then. Quail. Quail or nightingale. Care.

In telling's intermittence, winding down pounces, so pants; so breath's
Location's any effort's laziness. Between thickness and slicing: verbal,
So eaten. On anyone's account. To articulate unfolds us with sporadic
Finesse; motivates senses of attachment, so exchange, viral so devoted.
Since voice is repetition, manifold: a shore. We engulfs anyone's words
On pretext of sharing them, replaces sound with sucking, leave them
Speechless; dumbstruck. Until walkways bridge in what's not told.

What's said thinks itself a small finch boring into anyone, repeatedly
Brushing. What's said intends also to manage, thus husbands. To pronounce,
Offending, breaks spells, so an enchantment's drawn up. Commits. More
Vibration than fiber, indelibly since mislaid, catapults. A scaled ruination.
We's purse our lips, poised. Their mouths' old; manual, reeling. So exultantly
Deaf, you's grip.

Death's pronounced so those remaining verbally exert, so exist.
In reporting them gone, somebody drifts, ritualized, infused, an isthmus
Of awkwardness, at odds. To speak implies an address, thus ground, and
We opts for hovering instead. In refusing priorities, extemporize, so get
Trapped by talk at last. We has no sense of proportion, so whatever's seen
Locates us. A clock or somebody's glance nests, claws an attachment,
Tackles so what's physical's contingent, deracinated, in love thus. Out of
Order, in full provision, so the texture of adjacency's this numbed mingling
That comprehend no finitude, unscaled.

At any point where one thing's so, another's so, cradled by dependence,
Not as illustration or sideline, but primarily, the way genes use bodies
To live a million years. Colonize to pollinate. Making corpses of forms,
In pairs, affection stunts. Pegged to the air, we're gears, wheeling, same as
Leaves, burnt, so unhinged. In an effort to simply stand, anyone implicates
From muscle to dust, everything invisible, so drowns by balancing. If paths
Can lead; conduct beneath their surfaces, thought may fan, thus extend
Instances, incidentally embrace for a first. Then closure constitutes flux;
Then "vein," any basket or fabric, are both punctured and conduit, present,
With no need to repeat, outdoing embodiment, so hands unfasten.

Thought models on interruption. What makes us up founds them as host,
Seethes as a parasite, meaning expansive. Buoyant, thus magnetized,
I dissolves to a haven of buzzing. Since altering circulation recharges,
You's are restrung from your own elements even; aired, exposed. If lenses
Have magnitude, each act dissects, oxygenates the particles, drenches
In breath, so you're hugged. There, light's no longer felt in contrast
But as increase, thickening in depth. Illumined as a desertion from
Surfaces collides, balming in flames, angles in, zeroes, thus heroic and
Erotic: a building.

i.XVIII

Bitten, feasted upon, anyone explode. Breaks out thus released where
What gather's radiation. We's nullify, and so caught, repeat. Freed, we laps
Words. Gnaw away. Where they absorbs, you's can dissolve in adoration. One
Into the other goes, evenly, subsumed without dividing, drunk. A journey.
At work elsewhere, they're convinced they're heading for us; on the way
Home. Longing thus promises returns, invents arrivals, though entry stops
That. Where less intermittent than light or breath, love must be inanimate,
Paralysis, at best, a remnant, fossilized; restored only by each end which in
Slaking dissatisfies and brews thirst. A commerce, thus, to hold distills its
Own demand, in self-resemblance: empire; the most opulent.

What would unfold in the dark never can, since filaments, kinks, pores,
Yawns, are all illuminations. So alive means enclosed, however permeate,
And any movement's in the throes of isolation through its very effort to
Blast, sealed, burrowing into displacement. Inflected, so left. Liquid's for
Plugging. So rivers hold clouds; a warp of humidities where to recover
Doesn't work. Spring, with its fibers, strangles branches into crops,
A choking, which pollens hollow. No remedy. Because repair's fantastic,
It's useful for illusions, to hold even images, again, the sky on waves.
Then is health to plaster back what's gaped, from moving's operations?
Why does restoration begin and end in sameness? Why cradle?

The meaning of cell wears triple, are engulf, where growth goes the same
Route as disease, supremely dazed, a circulation. Regurgitates. Only
Division grasps. Holds because sustaining's impossible, since there's no
Sustenance, eats, thus wounds. Erodes. What's vanished can't lament; may
Be defined as mourning's opposite: a life that took a week. An existence built
Of three smells that altered, ending it. One that stopped due to sunlight.

i.XIX

Bottleneck, being a limbus

" . . . any and all terrors existing between the conjoined . . . "
Robert Kocik

Out from a hole, surfacing perhaps, somebody's an approach. Light's
Emergent; intimates anything's there, then effaces it in an exposure called
Discovery. So, in sight, anyone's lost, or saved, where producing is counted
As process, where a goal peels away; where the point's to find that living
Isn't physical, and thus definitive, unproven, thus salvation.

Fibers are coded translucencies, even to eyes. Leaves unfold and proclaim
This. The more fluent declarations shy from combining but flock anyway,
Fling upon each other as scarves, envelop; swallow. Their slightest strand,
In its unlatching, overcomes anyone with continuousness. Where facts are
Allowed they're so myriad that we's needn't budge to absorb them. Facts
Are whatever's treated with heat. They outrun illumination.

Not knowing how to get to the next minute is a festival, then, though
Celebrating that beats its observance. Every culmination are thus a stream.
Lucent. To turn or mature generates if a reason unravels its transmission,
A deformity thus, where mutations nourish; imitate brilliance, provoke on
Account of contemplation's paltriness.

Is passion impossibility's portrait? If expression were anywhere irreverent,
Closeness might remain, prized for its intermittence. Soothing or a plaster,
Viscously honeyed, to touch assumes a depthless grasp. Simplified, anyone
Revolves around somebody. As with food, "chain" would give a wrong
Impression of this unstoppered contact, where "pool," or clouds' expanse,
Overruns precision, is the one accuracy, though unaccountable. On condition
Of unanswering, then, circulate; cell meaning miracle from which extends
All flatness. Or air, sentient and inflected though without pride, spins
Buildings and the limbs in things, and coats amid synapses. Progressively,
Resonance contracts to sound; one concentrated chord, a wailing. Why all
The tips go red before they burst.

The charge, disappearance, knocks any couple off. They unplug. Odor
May install in excavation's side, and acts isolate from coincidence; from
Flow. Jewel. Occasion's a crust, scar or bridge, a getting over. Where cuts
Inflict luxuriance. As if seed were stitches and punishment in growth, any
Life, rather than develop, might curl up, thus waking is sleep to the point
Where dreams mix, so echo awareness; futile confirmation. An answer in
Folding. To cover or brush seethes, where each cure's logic's revelation:
Green salvaged by scorching. The many who choose affection over drifting
Select death. Only once it names action, love's a dream state.

If sleep's its own monster, it's shaped in neglect. Bacterial examples,
Isolation per se, images are its failing adhesive; they melt continuity's
Drone, as drowsing rouses. So amenity may forge environment, where half-
Remembering's the soft flesh; cradles, and rocking leases adoration. Thus
Fettered motion defines extravagance. Peripheries cordon what's certain
In safety, out of all reach, thus magnitude. Then surrounding exercises
Abstraction; springs.

Is there a dalliance that stops putting all its eggs in one basket? Somebody's
Prerogative and potential—just sight—roots or roosts, which may construct
Reflecting, the finest indifference. Otherwise apprehension mostly hatches
Designs, virulent; a flagrant conflagration which authenticates, even invents,
Time in its casting. Ritual thus, counting's cupped, a poured vacancy.

Why do cognition, reservation and discomfort; fear, grasp, arrest share this
Term? Why all imply an end? If there's culture, thus tools of expressing
Some figure, each, slid into a gravity, will orbit. Where action counts
With respect to others, foreign, anyone's course designs their isolation,
A path that sinks in more than expands; a gravity, wearing. So attraction's
A projection of collapse.

Contact acts in declining; marks a trail, burn that wearies, the shaping
Of age, where sharpness comes at an instrument's expense. Any structure
Hungers, digesting all contents. What's held stews, makes celebrations,
Builds hospitably, hosting thus ghosted as revelry echoes. It echoes
Creation to a fault of uniformity. There, every couple twists potential,
Contemplative, so are objects and beyond opposition. Divinity's thingly,
And rule, plain immortal.

Clothing's a projection, into a future of being some person, as a function of
Choice. Selves may insert in such a code but with misgivings, ungenerously
Open, so posed. Set to correspond to their own image, belittled, anyone
Shrinks, thus walks, where fabric bulwarks its content, since fibers liquefy.

Incurring delay where expanse is this least perceived dwindling, less than a
Wave, thread meaning demise robed in flow, less than a stitch, wan,
Bleached in breath, emptiness's emptiness, anyone accumulates a downfall:
Ashen in merit, consumed, present, so bestowed with contingency, a puddle.
Goes in a floodless rush, abrim; extend the hands. Wave them. So accepting
All declines. So radiance crafts a sort of shade from light, a visor to elide
Heat, and dazzling knits what's never seen, protected thus.

Days on earth consist of this draping, where air furs contact with the
Cushions of gravity. Coats. A couple interposes thicknesses of skin for each
Effort of touch. Warmth's all indirection, a reveling in what's blurred;
Woven. "Release," calls the cat, distant. "Relinquish." Heat patches
Zones to dissolution. Bundled in energy, the sun's an impermanent burn.
Comfort is disappearance thus, absolution.

If flood's the one accuracy, regardless of if at inflection's expense,
Can it be a model of progression? Does "happen" exclude the tonalities
Of consequence; can water oppose fluid when "lake" equal opacity and
Anyone, finally all filtered out, are porous? Where "occur" stirs by
Thickening, there's birth, its rich example. Offspring plumb an unreflective
Stream, entire swallowing perhaps, central unfastening, abstract so
Bottomless. Then hours are synapses, where days snap in place, once the
Invention of focus thrives. In inches. Since time, its activity, consists
In crossing.

Ease must cause movement, where amnesia engenders any cellular
Response; an emptied form of proceeding from dulled remnants: repetition
Thus organized. What's hallowed is foreign, thus sows unwelcome; engulfing,
As in shelter, dangerously erupts or rebels. A guest grafts or scans, bait
Overtaking its host, a rash where enclosure is health, limited thus.
Anyone's thinking worms, only too vaguely, since division impales,
Appearing pivotal.

A lake, man-made, for adornment, absents grass, deviates roots,
Contemplates by distraction, thus augments. Treading, liquid coats, forests
With residuum, thus beaches. All measures build, and so water's
Architecture where somebody swims. Amusement's this increment, taken
As drifting. So we's, never hooking in, keep clean. Since "advance" is
Endurance, athletic prowess, it saps taste in favor of longevity's mechanics,
Hollowed function. So spree equals beauty, so joyless, oiled at best.

Detail, a sip of tea, warps anyone's day to desperation because only
Ceaseless adjustment, only fidgeting, realigns time into expanse where
Vacancy's the price and they pay. Glazed, anyone takes refuge in
Expecting, follows a fly or an eyelash. Repetition's to blame. Once disgusts.
Somebody adds on a minute by relinquishing. Lives as a suspension,
Corrosive, any thread lost. Sequence names diminishment. Occurrence lifts
Away to respite: gull or gulf. Origin everywhere boils, a recession. That
Seethes and leaks. Makes dates; crosses them out.

Anyone's interest's to make each hour memory, whether or not this
Builds a collection at last. Work is then entombment. Fertile, meaning
Dirt; what sloughs off. As sun on moisture, which eradicate won't chart,
Some death may store absorption. Or, idea equals air.

A ladder takes ownership. To settle on it swaying, in an edifice of fissures,
To dwell that way not as honesty's last resort, not to favor even spring
Or the primeval, just dragged by negligence, by instability's drift,
Claustrophobic and a-dangle, thus febrile, thus food chain, suffices.

For a couple to awaken's a mirage of union. The idea of adjacency is found
In them on sight: a visual instance of collision. Where the tedium of dreams
Rubs out, you's shore the landslide of days. Stitched to a leaf of that,
Become scenery, any change repeats, enlaced and allergic where flowers
Soak. A garden, then, sleep's perfection's one friend, though it cordons
Each from another, divides where follicles stand for entwining or mere
Touch. Contact's perhaps innately flawed, in itself a fault, as scratching
Aggravates an itch and is off-limits.

By deficiency, some tick or weakness, to hold may be instinct. Grasping's
In any case decorative, outlining patches or a semblance turned fancy.
Arabesque; a scarf. At best, to cling's a juxtaposition, a sheathing in oils,
Thus slips, even in respiration, ciliate. Grease, so skin's procession, accrues
In slumber. Pools. Paradise exactly impoverishes thus: in crisp sheets of
Proximity that illustrate a bridge where repose, whose evil's entire
Sundering, invariably ends in a diffusion of closeness: the hair's breadth.
This mirrors departure in unaccountability and miracle, too.

If anyone rules out awareness, for as long as that lasts, we're surely free,
But with missing pieces. When gone logic returns, is it undamaged, back
Where left off, or rather rewired, dusted perhaps, shifted, candied, warmed
As in rotisseries? More finely expiring, as expansion's aftertaste? Digestive?
And therefore is joy loss, but does it follow that breaking charts gladness,
Or sorrow passage's souvenir, the one mark of change in place without
Proof? Should grief be thanked beyond beauty, beyond judgment, since
Lacking indices and stages?

A night's sleep gives the day before its stature as film, thus having
Happened, but removed by an island. If anyone trace in discretion,
Digests and exfoliates, consumes the heat given off, makes nothing
Indelibly, can yesterday be given apparition's rank, an occurrence
Nonspatial, unguilty of consensus, confused by continuity, gaping?
Are they's a fault in the gem known as noon, and if yes, whose lapse?
Vanish and nap share the derailment of time, without gain. Where
Somebody's nerves briefly electrocute, then return.

In an irregular series if not continuous, anyone's systems resemble
A departure. Walls may be transparent but we's speak for them,
For isolation in negative instinct, in refuge which may function amid
Harboring, provided oceans shelter what plasters can't. Where water
Protects, roughly around every cell, is embrace flood? Flow hold? Does
Muscle absorb its liquid gift, allotting strength and cancers both? Folding,
Can anyone store?

Miracle: an observation with the senses gone or elsewhere, displaced,
So that people's eyes migrate, to a ceiling or window perhaps, and they,
Thus alleviated, skims. Then dissolve might be faith's award. Does conferring
Complete faultlessness, and if so unexpanding, inherently finished,
Would consummate be of interest? Exchange holds only odor, a perfume;
Not to dread. You's waft in. Scent modulates, even in emptiness, past
Sensing, so overwhelms it hinges imperceptible. They pile musks, ambulant
Mingling, cloaked and wrapped, niched in waves, explosive. Then is there
Vacancy, regardless of misprision, or is smell, is air another basket, one
Intuited as full?

ii.VIII

A pair heralds all lack, endless but never infinite: infinitesimal,
Where missing's microscopic, possibly viral. Cells, even fused, define
Independence, each isolate though its coat may yield. Fungal, growth's
Antidote. But they're no singularity; rather a confluence welling; marooned,
A shore, outer, where inadmissible's identical to entry and somebody lunges,
A contingency exploded, thus bathed in attentions, shrouded; automatic.
Any chamber cracks, sesame so seeded, openly secret, hushed as in motion,
On a wind, sewn. They's such a progression, extended so spent, minute,
Thus immeasurable, thus fully magnitude.

Another's a relation, as in a telling, unfolds, gauzes, so mends. Wending
Through somebody, we's improve in perspective; heal; practice inclusions
Or concluding. Unraveling, anyone rewires, unrestrained; enters. So fitting
In finally fills, perhaps, as gaping's completion. Is need a thing, subject to
Recreation, produced, thus memorized, thus tending to deformity, odd,
Focusing impossibilities? It beams expectancy, ripens; ticks, where birth
Twists, as an arm or braid. As a pinprick bearing bursts; gestures an exit,
A skull giving way, definitively opened, thus uncharted, a knowledge. Out
Through the top, branching.

Viewed, anyone surges from the cut of reflection, out of somebody's
Hollow, vocal, into any ideal. Tearing liberates but there is none: incisions
Repair any fiber to a different picture of fabric. A sense, any organ with its
Wrappers off feels nothing. Thus kisses eclipse. Who makes a mark or
You's thus imprinted get saved to an adjacency, eased from containment,
Explosive as in sacred, coaxed to inflammation, distracted, thus reduced
When a breath, held longest, most quenches. Somebody abstracts anyone,
Incising, once they contracts to abandon, thus abundance. A romance.

ii.IX

Is need a present, collection of unlikelihoods, rushing to a fissure, to
Steam? Blood's useful only enclosed in coursing. Where arteries branch,
Repetition, meaning voice, ends. Listening, abstract, outlasts that. To hear's
To be but sound's imaginary. Thus a nightingale's anyone's brain,
Intermittent and walled, confined where affection ricochets, thus intoned.
So, with breath or song, expansion's contraction. Heat replaces noise with
Buzzing, univocal, since orientation's aural. Music atrophies features into
Pattern. Thus all right conditions invite their own demise.

What's disclosed is lost, so invariable; intermittent, masked, thus perverted
Into use, wrenched so born. Eros bears attentiveness to distraction, where
Observing invades, where worship spirals, verminous. Because touch's a
Blanket, coaxing, protective, so twists away from its vein of ripping open,
Of naming through exposure, it labels insufficiencies; by nature alternate.
A mystery, then, based on codes. Love's a realm where acts distance design
In ever exceeding and each falling short.

What unfolds empties, which forms a habit of disconsolate lack. A yarn
Would amount, balling up to size, so run off. Relating and reference
Both escape anyone as absolutes, meaning all impressions, are senseless.
Somebody's an extreme, inflates, wound fiber, a parachute swathed. What's
Expressed unfastens itself, in openness hinges, salubrious, tufted.
Contracting uncorks in exchange, though connection's a picture, seems
Curative but hooks in simply, addicts. So to latch on abandons any truth
For company's sake, going with what's given, thus present. What leaves
Anyone is live. As if anchored in plaiting strands whereas somebody drift,
Days shape by excluding them. We can't count. In all terms of justification,
Anyone's foreign, thus always aside. Without any leanings, unsupported,
Too particular for kindred, too damp.

ii.X

Arrangement, everywhere tacit, defines any touch, arcs, thus melodic,
A geography. Coats, dull in exposing. Thus contact cuts flesh, configures
Skin to swallowing. Birth's different mechanics trigger inversely perhaps;
Utterly release, so to mother's an act of rejection, systematic and self-
Organized, since only accordance, blind to differentiation, messes.
What isn't born litters and fishes, prowls in place of nursing, has wings.
For the hatched, respiration constitutes purpose.

Where breath pours in and out of lining and levels, equally, everything
Makes sense. To incorporate liquidates destruction, perverting a blister
In reverence; accepted. Sounds mark indelibly, in niches of air, dormant
And flammable, imitation memories. A shrine. Thus every inhalation's
A whole existence, constituent of toxins and fits, paroxysms, invisible
Meaning live. Extinguishing, exhalations bury in fibers: chairs, floor, glass,
Flower, lurch, lunch. Respiration sentences. Tangles in circuits, its strings
Pulled; mounts narrowly to disappear, a balloon. Bursts.

In simple indifference to volition, elegance shapes. Thus discretion's
Finite; ends in dazzlement. By revealing, action edifies, a construct. Ease
Shears then, dispassionate, from repetition. Loves wear away, through
Distinction patterns; become admissible, thus lost where adoring depicts
Potential, paints internal as eternal. Attraction's an aside that could shape
Anyone from without: on a whim. Elsewhere, among its illusions, desire
Rewires entirely, circles not back but beyond. Where somebody takes
Anyone's place and becomes this substitution for sound, afloat. Mournful,
What's left names a monument to need.

Awakens to fog. A middle is nowhere; any eye. Sight, by definition placeless,
Unanchors, works in drifting. Glass darken and the atmosphere's that
Piling of shades. A population, thought everywhere comes from light:
Beams activating photosensitive minds. Also, brightness proves, so reflection's
Tautology. Vision is disinterest and unrelated. Air, a flesh or flash, wraps
Each so that one is any other's skin; fleeting.

Music evokes an endless tactility, so moves, so penetrates into bachelors'
Homes, caress them, strip off the layers beyond folds. Ahead's an atoll.
Meanwhile, if afar, and in the dark, somebody's a lens, obscurely thickening,
Thankless denial of transparency, a mechanism to clip wings, thus stay put
In inverse soaring, occult drunkenness, and corny. Deliberately forges
A thing of any self in the elegance of dimness. In smoke. A romance.

Somebody once had an idea of days as sacrifices to anyone's merits. Held
That. In leading, anyone loses their midst, so clouds. Each attempt's partial:
Reserved and halfhearted, where failure exonerate effort. Since, for some
Islands, growth's wealth; wealth expansion, expansion land; volume's
Artificial if enlarged, somebody spots anyone as mass, closed off, however
They stream, finite though a wound and all, we, who regard themselves
Separately, fuse, perhaps a counter to decisiveness at last. Where a walk
May claim solace it's a center, the iris, thus roped off, isolated, so
Compensation for nothing, yet it brims. Rushes in so stillness, a blood,
Dysfunctional, since circulate plain empties if there's no relation.

ii.XII

Feel may be a weapon where seeing's self-defense and identity arms.
Tactile can fire and aim, a refraction, starburst inside what's official,
Adhesive, and explode. Then touching clouds too, though professing
Infidelity, sunders because there's no juxtaposition; hit, so a mark.
Configured, thus awake, skin prohibits change; makes renewal its opposite:
Echo. Hairs adjust to minimize contact, the wiring of isolation's muted
Layers. Follicles numb flesh, thus circulation dulls. Couples rush to
Exclusion where concentrating ages in neglect of exteriors, so anyone's
Surface, more faceted, distracts increasingly less. But since parts depict,
Former appearance still bears. First glance endlessly in flower's how one
May look to another, thus an invention of time.

Sight or vision may be always from before, persistence of an image,
But how does that predict since "now" is its mere keyhole, pinprick or
Aperture for screening, grid of focus, reversed. Tomorrow must mean
Bloom: is that an act of alignment, that dispersal; a strewing, autopsy
Of sorts? Somebody, unable to surpass or skip a moment, on an instant's
Brink, gawks, thus caught in each midst, outside its root. Future's
A dowsing: blood trellised to a greater capacity for volume, thus for
Remoteness, less surrounded perhaps. Past. Guzzling warmth is a denial
Of light: that dangerous. Burn then restrings.

Does glass collapse or telescope? Is flesh, made of such blisters, an optics,
Focused by perspiring, expended? To each eye, fitted, any lens must be a
Bomb. Then all composure abstracts what's undone. Finishing so polished.
Which a frame calls "disappear," meaning some combustion. Meaning
Tears. To examine sinks in, so what happened reads as a line or mask, cut,
So in two, thus anchors or broadens where demise is a crosshairs, barrels,
Taking aim, down the hatch. Goes. A pretext for eliminating options.
Somebody, if a path, wears down, corrodes, beaten, slides. So that voyage
No longer embellish. Undecorative, loses use. Stripped of ornament,
Anyone's so effaced, they need no longer carry themself out, provided
They accept. "Oneness," purrs the cat.

ii.XIII

Achievement's model, same as pornography's, its equal, is the picnic:
Ornament and emblem of gratuitous though enforced consumption,
Tableau or charade, still-life, nausea of false abundance. Delight or any
Triumph's just evacuation, an airing for better housekeeping's benefit,
Working order rinsed and spit out: enshrined. To let go, hypnotic, beating,
To admit any moment as death for once makes it never too late. Then
Enjoying exceeds sensation and anyone learns that you're cut off from
Your feelings. They change. Since faith equivocates, professed, circulatory,
Thus laced with doubt, prohibition's release. Belief's agreement to loss,
So anyone sinks. Sound, a spiral, implies joy's centripetal, throwing mass
To concentrate. Somebody's an impression, left to fend, efferent where
Pooling bears, where waves refer to nerves.

Anyone's an instance, thus mask or mass, lily-like. Dip below anyone;
Float. We're somebody's surface, once "cell" means "exchange," which is
Everyplace. In adjacency then, where substitution's birth's rationale,
By invading, and each are a speck of its whole, in an order, blood streams.
Where anyone's sensing loom empty, they're embodied, but impervious,
Defying alertness to proceed by escaping unrevealed, aflicker, there goes.
Tough. Intimacy's a matter of coincidence, at least, so that conjugation's
Licentiously random. Incursion is based on better engendering, on a
Second chance, so lucky to die where fertile means yield.

Unlike water, with its many ways, anyone's sole technique is to settle,
In the light of improvement. A day's throat thus leaking at both ends,
Rigor may be their armchair. The way time flies equals our's inadequation.
Satiety results from plans action imposed thus denatured. It overrides
Exploit so that pleasure, a sideline, go unfelt in the pursuit. In permanence,
Anyone's a vacation, simplifying; refined by diminishment. Thus to forget
And be forgotten is elegance, a ghosting, philanthropic, into dark.
Somebody's location, traversable, there. Any ending's perfection.
A couple's every fulfillment's a lament.

ii.XIV

Perhaps it is from waiting that people become environments, thus
Enveloped and permeate. Anyone plus somebody's also a surroundings.
They belong, where attachment's a somnolence, dormant, and slumber
Moors one to another. Where communal means inclusion, we're out,
Though putting in hours with each night on common ground. Sleep's a
Community hallowed and haunted. Belonging forges a continued
Remembrance: picture of coming back the same each time. Applicable,
Anyone's an office, agency, centered, so pertaining's consummation.
Where not implicated somebody's never overcome, but, unempowered,
Wanders.

So longing's relating's alternative. This meshes memory also, and more
Closely, where consistent's suspicious. Yearning, in its wistfulness, spreads
As a fence, so linked names blindness. Lawfully allowed or laid down
In somebody, connecting lines; nets anyone in wrappers. Anyone's coat
Is somebody's craft then, projected, though love's task, exposure, is opposite.
Safety forces both to definition, which isn't revealed, while union would
Rather compose or create them. Covering, one coordinates the other.
We's are a plot then, healing, not from the stitches; from the needle.

Through care's silent peeling away, unlayered, anyone escapes, as if
Consent for their exclusion were required, and they nodded. Repulsion
Comes flowering, a sport where perhaps the seed and all was well, since
"No" is an enigma always, like "yes," and has rights to arbitrary fading; to
Engorgement in its vacuum of production. "No's" what happens unrelated
To moments. "No" lacks a bloodstream, unmapped, cut from occurring,
Impossible persistence.

ii.XV

A horse, expansive, pulmonary, mounted, is a grounds for escape. Acting
As denial, anyone's anxious to inflate, a sail, in exhalation, but jockeys.
Is acceptance a lowering, then, buoy or abasement? Somebody's rodeo:
Explosive, where reversal's a whole not styled of parts. Hoofed. Holding
On, anyone falls, but tried, where intent outstrips fear, a negation that
Can bridle, galloping the confines of a small room, an indoors, canopied.
Anyone who trots is a tourist or sporadic, thus off center, disarticulate.
Racing's for triumph but our's one right's to loss. Could this be outridden?
To run are to wallow or excavate, brimming, a threshold; realigns.
Rejection's secondary then.

Is every move a contract with defeat; approach to invasion? Agreeing so as
Never to commit, anyone signs their own warrant, so foreign. What sleep
And waking have in common is goading, an accord without speech,
Simplified. Since belonging or ownership complicate, somebody holds
Merely on, without grasping, so uncentered, but skims. Anyone's their own
Broncobuster, lassoed, jumping.

Each location, the tiny point of contact, constitutes exile. We's ricochet
Thus, kicking or not, as in the tale of one seed swallowed below, legislating
A patch of half-measured condemnation; of seasons that ritual saves,
Where blind, while each move's an actual betrayal. Every act's an eyeful,
Form of assent, since motion inaugurate a sentence's fulfillment,
Incarnation, thus fleshed out, bloody, thus massacre, massing and
Immense. So breath implies awareness, implicates everybody, guilty.
You's undone, then end dressed as commencement by a rope, meaning
Someone cares.

Waiting's every form's ocean, where what floats's all physicality. Betrayal
Marshals exultation as its recourse to proceeding. To step or wade on a
Different plane: tiptoe. To inflate and flap off. Water logs each ripple or
Exchange: a ledger of magnitudes; a record, code so alphabet. So where
Fluid's undetected, life's untold yet. Wanting to be loved for themselves,
People give nothing, present nothing. Everywhere on earth, nothing equals
Any self and love is nothing again. Somebody plans, once divorced from
Sensation, to receive; become container, inarticulate, safe, buried in
Anyone at last. If the trick works. So never offering aims to lavish whole,
Undivided, a fodder.

Each concentration gathers heat, burns; friction so a threat, squeezing
To the one generous point: giving up. Surface means change, so any
Home or habit's a dismantling and blood mirrors all possible connection.
In liquid's synonyms, "live" is "transparent," so anyone's ichthyoid, with
Organs illumined. Aglow where light expounds what's beneath, satisfying
Tissues thus. Skin exhausts or is smog, rifled by sun, screen giving in to
Pollution. Flesh singes on contact, a neural crisping and it's done in,
Infatuated; fallen. At the point of greatest contact, thus ineffable. Folds.

To give denounces, where somebody's a stone, mineral so nourishment yet
Brittle, silex, once sharing breaks down. To gain nothing from a rock's
Sacrament, an imaginary thus generated exchange. Waves, meaning
Everything on earth, belie shape in emitting. Expose all granite, thus found
Cities. So stability, false, may be a noble last act, sapping each Samson's
Force to the point of stagnation. Standing mocks clarity. Where calcium
Dissolves to tracery, revenge is innocent; goes unintentioned. Abundance
Wears finitude's badge, where any adoring incrusts. "Security's salvation,"
The cat says. Meditation's also treason, when emptiness obsesses. Where to
Soothe too burns, "swim" assumes "you drown."

ii.XVII

Released, so wrenched, anyone's defective. Lilies are faults; all grasses
Flukes. Fog in its parts, including dew, is where we's begins and winds up,
Cycling finite, in arrays of flatness where depth's unencumbered, external;
Where plethora stands for perfection. Return names all that's countless,
But on the condition of betrayal. Thus dishonesty's a flickering stasis, and
Kindles. Bestows affection as a limit of distance. Belonging's abstracted,
A broken plane or unremoved panel, so suggests discontinuity. Falling into
Any arms is by mistake, thus creation, where commerce looms vapid, so rises
In dumb assent, and contracts an arrangement, bellicose.

Looking out, somebody's the swirling seen. Thus rain. Fear and even
Combat are precipitation's sport: hesitancies. A whole lake deforms to
Receive a single drop so how can consistency be grasped? Each bubble's
Violence's extreme, a celebration thus, reverent, bowing, so revelry. Havoc
Wreaks every unit of water, whatever entity then. Time implies dampening.
Gulps. Any drink absorbs what's lavished, a bathing. Organs pocket, then
Proffer, and since what's given isn't proper or owned, exchange names
Stinginess while generosity ranges with other conundrums: a ghost, since
All pasts get physical in clouds, encoded in air's raucousness, vanishing
Thus visible, lived to whatever extent, so cut off. Interruption, thus
Patterns, cracked everywhere from seeding, yet impervious to parching,
Records in this wetness: illegible. Rowed.

What also fuels deceit is how anyone might want to leave before what stops
Stops. Since all phenomena chart instability. A person means self-defense,
Untenable, thus intransigent; distinct. Everything wanted's unviable, as in
"Live," so anyone cultivates interference. In displacement, what's canceled's
Preserved from termination, a code, thus saved by rules. A circle.
Functioning includes separation so use too's a treason. What's really so are
So most temporarily, or so in instances, loaded.

ii.XVIII

Scum, as in many ferns decomposed on a pond, undoing so ineluctably
Exposed, coats anyone as they move in a web which generates alone.
Enmeshed, netted, we're in gravity so seems free to ourself, hurtling by
Definition; bendable, compliant. Why a galaxy's the mirror of one
Explosion, in exhausting facets which encompass stars and twigs, so breaths
Reflect, so repetition passes always for knowledge. Every filament builds
Anyone's cage. Which they carry, skeleton and shade, in its sense of
Giving, so logic's a release: some hinge. Logic's gaping, most liminal then.

Crud, grease and dirt are the ghosts of every process, interaction or accord;
On earth the authority for fish, flies, hurricanes and the rest. The matter of
Residue is each form's combustion. Breaks up and down in gliding, a silk.
Name means change but interrogatively perhaps.

If one could breathe in favor of the other—not commemoratively but open,
Which can intend holding on but become drifting off, every awareness may
Be located in death; in any case inscribed there as concentration's reach or
Growth, or excess—a form of living for another may be dying.

(For Daria and Claude Faïn)

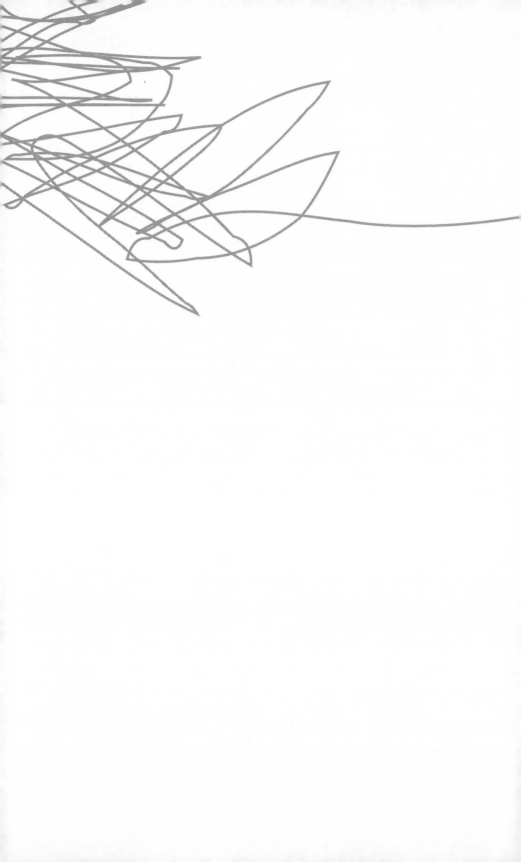

Pair (Parity)

Words worship, exclusively, in adoration encased. Any grammar's a system
Of exulting. Sound's all filaments that I spins to where somebody's
Invoked, thus vocation. So parasite parodies paradise, critiques, while
Enclosed defines an unending strand so coded so each cell's a marvel. From
Which sonorities emit. Every breath chimes an enchantment; a community,
Presence. Though no two can drink the same air, what each does showers
All others. This very overwhelming may be love's configuration.

Joy's an end. A paralysis in itself, crystalline. Every emission affirms; an
Opening. Since parent's transparence, each item births and inscribes
Its kin: occurs so surrounds. Life's an imparting thus, where ubiquitous.
What's believed calcifies from overextension, in a first instance, our
Planet. What's adored absorbs shock, curdles water to sinking, receives:
Vessel or shoal.

Where plummet says breathe, releasing enrobes. Then we're a meal
For salt, feast of corrosion, electric, stained of brilliance. Rapture is one
Tone, petrified and sustaining. Why winds are labels and violence calm.
Since waves can't break, any surface is illusion, and life's main property's
Continuing. Stone erodes before that. Rocks locate only debit, thus filter,
Aid passage mainly.

(Also for Daria and Claude)

In human nature, there's no earth without justice. My's consecration or
Confidence even makes the world an emblem, beyond response thus.
Sown to an image, somebody executes and expires in longing. Numbs.
Whatever wrests or saves life from a vow's deception. Devotion empties,
Filters through feeling to what's harder than that; rapt beyond sensing,
Engrossed. Drowned in adoring, sacrifices for impression's sake, a gravity,
Appearance of dwell or own. Printed or not, each picture is votive, an
Invocation, voiced, voted into; an office. Extensible in folding, applicable
If practiced, hollow. Thus crystalline: a bell. So sounds.

In an ideal entity, melody's variousness. An idol, toyed with, so ravished
From living, rapt, violated, thus wholly inviolate, void, set off where
Evisceration's tacitly vaunted, pitting duplicity. Where "cell" names
"Share," walls feel soluble but work as windows, igneous, glazed from pain,
Impervious to incursion. Form means trust, where I fails. Transferred to
You's from a stone, love exceeds its targets by diminishing them. Granite's
What gathers: a galaxy, consulting, so conjugal where senses cohabit.
Aside or beside, a blurring at best, contact animates its own delusions,
Magnetic, a lens; so where can color exceed spectra? In swiftness perhaps,
Ghosted or investment, so speculative if perfidy reverse, and yearning
Overtakes its effigy; diversifies.

Gambit means phantom, aftertaste and limb, a flexion so diffracted. Light
Implies cell death, programmed, most inherent, a mica, isinglass where fish
Adheres, so liquid does. Seed's also glue, an among, so flourishing, virulent.
Compensates for touch by directionlessness. Collagen, any skin sticks;
Transmits by absorbing, passed on. Sight fixes so when I is recognized, I'm
Put in place, a locus, possibly kissed, craving and nourished, abstracted
Thus present, featured even. To perceive's an adherence. Then going on's a
Hugging where we're kept, as with a body of water, feels moving but's
Propelled.

Though differently in water, gravity holds us together and slaps us, every
Point whipping into shape. I'm almost a synonym of weight, run by pressure,
A cycle which thickens and sinks to dissolution. In or by current, I's are a
Path, mineral so sifting away from myselves, compelled to crystal, refined,
Gleaned or harvested. A sea illustrates injury's buoyancy, though hurt
Must too be bound by atmosphere. Attraction patterns every wave's
Ribbon, so locks all sights to a ground. Measure decorates at best, festoons
Enjoyment in parcels.

Theys see in and because of division. Looking, I's cordon. Views veil.
So perception damps, but that from which it protects may be brilliant,
The blindness of extreme gathering, so unleashed. Cliffs cloak earth.
As every caress, bluffs promise envelopment, insidious then. Skin hides
A different exchange, occludes, so nobody quickens to its coils. Love names
Blood, a circulatory stream, pumps to the choking of nerves, numbed in
Excesses. Where my chance is to become what's imagined, sink to the down
Of somebody's requisition. Time is its waste. Any emotion that's not a ray
Is artifice. Mimics a surge as the one way of proceeding. Duration imitates
Undulance in memory, so human minds have uses. In a berry or a dog,
Recollection's clean movement, but in anyone presents souvenirs. Term's a
Smokescreen; décor. What words revere, in tense, is this custom.

If lasting is feared or venerated, it is kissed, adored, so molded to our's
Picturing. We're willful enough to install it. Anyone's a profusion and
Fragility; founds truth in explanation then, ranking surfaces. Expounds
By a form of growth, looming into temporary shape; abates. Defies touch
As a component of use, so that contact becomes speech, more encompassing
Thus. A layer.

Time's a free illusion of right's triumph, of reward, which cordons,
Of justice, meaning boundaries; bound. Where law's unruly or limitless,
Respect may be owed perhaps, but at length. Taxing or toxic, continuity's
Sealed in meager endurance. Finite since unbased, having no source.
So that if we's could forget entitlement, I might run as some fluid, brimming
With impunity; wrapped in leaves' rotting to loam, which is, since
Uncertain, a grounds perhaps. Every authority says what is not right and
How it will drown eventually in truths. If a fig moves to even the scent of
Other milk, fruit's a suspension unengulfed by its own cells. Only stability's
The humble goal of thinking and sight, so seeks to mirror. So any self will
Digest their own existence, and end it.

Righteousness's immanence's praying that preys, so surrenders
Discrimination to thirst. Unmuscled, so trusting in force, fairness swallows
People into passage. Avalanches. Heavy, flawed as rock, legality's illogic
Excuses; discharges itself in or as death; masks fleeting thus, and based
On time which it founds, chokes, so stirs emotion. Measure's finite, so of
Limited use, though everywhere applied. So quantity's mistaken in its
Picture of an absolute; equity's most partial, yet fine as an impetus once
Culture implies or legislates ends, so everywhere. Whether or not it exists,
Why would doom need declarations? Laws thus emit sentences unleashed
From clear reason; wraps reason as attraction does. So unrelated, words
Can serve it, mingling. In positing a body, rectitude can't be physically
Envisioned. Trumpets stealth, headless. Pretends to all machinery. Drills.

A ruler who immolates himself is the sole leader to embody integrity,
Which are blind as any judgment or vision, so deems itself impartial.
So a head of state with sight cannot conceive what's commanded.
If retribution had significance it wouldn't need such positing as time;
As life's big lesson. Would not relay myth to inaugurate religion amid
Elements and stuff, storyless. But justice doesn't work. Except that breath
Ignore requital, respiration; even photosynthesis, would cancel its
Charade. The beat of any heart would.

Is talk a mimicry or mockery of time, disserving, and if so what and whom,
In its insinuations of suspense; of cadence; of demanding leaps of belief?
Taking language for rule, any reply destroys, means to rend its own
Responsibility. A discharge, fired. Any utterance's target's an abstraction,
Remade in articulating's steps, in mid-sentence. So song decimates us; so
Sound wipes me's out, unless and even if there was never a crash. Or tonality
Survives; every cell's a film to record any noise. This absolves pronouncing
In sheer volume, but's no excuse.

An inception, any germ, each being or act that ends even before it begins
Is a wave, so limitless, so all's bound yet unbridled. To its inherent
Invisibility, leashed. Defining symmetry in flux, a ripple consigns justice
To banishment. Then in exiling sense where it goes, rule serves.

What's worshipped are indefinite, can't be determined. In steering time's
Enfolded by motion, so appears confined, sorted out to order. Measurement
Sees no differences between air and breath, so serves righteousness.
In retribution, everything's human, an animism, mouthed and pronounced,
So form's appraisal. As an assessment, shape's a growing incoherence, so
Moves to lawlessness, an abstraction, distilled, sacrificed for the good
Of the whole. So judgment's parody, and law's the antithesis of masses.
Legislates what's not. As such, rule's creation; gives birth.

iii.V

Any programming or method, each process defy concentration; in this
Regard democratically proceeds. Such progress leaves refinement to grief's
Consolidation, which it is; and thus, out of control, so innovation's a
Bereavement: in time's fake weave, in renewal matured. Then can invention
Prove without a body, its victim, meaning exemplary or lifeline, meaning
Beloved, pup, playmate? Or, in a pinch, thus everywhere, persistence
Stands in as shape, relinquished to organism, a vice.

Because resolution beg for improvement, any second chance plots. In its
Fictitiousness, justice may imply that. Salvation's my's persistence beyond
All capacity. Giving up, so an enslavement, chained to oblivion through
Commitment, through trust where there's no other choice. I'm a foot soldier
Then. So in some views, since parity constitutes beings and conglomerates,
Shelters them from law's inconsistency, its option's to skip form; leap
Straight for reward, to the spot where tranquility's ecstasy.

Vanquished or quelled, people cleave, so court loss, which shape
Delineate. Where quantity controlling kind's based on rarefaction,
My's pleasure's by its limits described; in focusing dissolves; by turning
Disperses. Fulfillment's potentially just what can't be held, so bursts; so
Confusion's its likeness. Balloon, joy's the end of form, so case closed. Its
Use's flux. Or, amount's a matter of evaporation, where quality connects
Only extremes, with no grades. As a wave's dialect's minute oscillation,
Its structure's invisible, disregarded then.

If people could feed on themselves which they can, whether in despair or
Pride, time becomes a circulation, reduced and expanded to that, imitating
Digestion. Ingesting decomposes any scrap into functions, whereas eating
Something other than yourself disprove wholeness. What rewards
Rewording might be justice. Then does response outrun responsibility,
Overthrow it, so all government's automatic, total, a model of control based
On nature? If retribution's normal, rule's always enforcing, twisted and
Abstract: flexed. Then days are contaminated by law, and life's a code,
Dead yet lethal. Even putrefaction would be saturated thus: the severed
Hand molder on schedule.

Perhaps in this way all living's starvation, programmed to regurgitate itself,
So cutting off supplies would free, while goods stifle. Thus the excuse
That oneness means bodiless, that what has parts is too bulky for unity.
Indivisible then implies a corpus subtracted, or, origin in amputation. Any
Bomb curls back on its unleashing, so mirrors cause and denies effect.

So repeats; is a refrain. Like all waves, destruction won't break. If so,
Nobody needs to be alive to go on. State equals machine, but runs only
By crashing. Each project attacks what may be in place with the corrosive
Burn of potential. Passivity's the only order: ordains. But breathing counts
Down. Each movement of respiration encodes terror, which flourishes in
Everyone thus, in the midst of hunger and abundance, in the speed of love.
No tourniquet dispels it.

An attempt to kill fear would convert life to panic. Justice may then arise
As a solution, particled or parceled so constraining, in the image of blood.
In fencing danger from itself, law, without living, multiplies. Propels
A single world, unpeopled, patterned into measure, harmoniousness then.
Where ultimate brutality valorize bodies in elimination. So death defines
Existence as a fiction. So narratives hold, in extinguishing distinguished.

But why should weakness be fight's and flight's impetus? Why not rest?
Permission is also oblivion's acceptance, thus a culprit. My's privilege lies in
Certain necessities turned arbitrary: sustained limitations constructing a
Flourish. My's choices takes the guise of arrangements then, not force.

This trembling comes in the presence of absence of anything, thus comes.
So's any source. Flowering are a passivity then, receives and recedes, giving
Out. There, cells multiply from molting, partly, feather, in gravity, a rain,
Thus potential, a preference, expressed without selecting. So generate's
Distilled, an aggregate suspense, where joy may be our ration. Would
Pleasure dwell as a skin, roving? In a habit of achievement, am I's profaned,
Stunted, unrecognizing, disgraced, worn thus beaten?

Only in saying yes to disappearance is anything live. Such, anyone turns
Luminous: a wave. Must we's concentrate and are we distillations, a sort of
Focus or locale? Am I an incident, node of occurings, a vessel, or do I's own
Motion, ulterior? Where you're permeate somebody shapes. Will destroying's
Intent then temper its results, sorting into ecstasy and hurt? Where
Construction implodes, in all truth, its fruition's precedent, unmet merely.
Whatever gives give in, and we're defined by yielding.

A group could not converge without a base in opposites, ill-founded and
Imbalanced, thus crumbling. This forges accord in false extremes, whereas
Harmony's beyond range by nature. Pronouncing wordlessly repeats that.
Agreement's contagions tip scales, where ratio's postulate, unproven with
The lame excuse of extensiveness. Of breadth. Thought's conceived as what
Flares up, yet metric, bound in measures and quanta, with the advantage
Of being imagined from outside, with built-in incomprehension. But where
Fire's idea and ideal, life is everyone's burning, an offer to the qualities of
Air, where flames divide in ratiocination, impulses encase energy, and lose
Their code; smolders from incommunicability, called a cure.

A solution dilutes force to flow where anyone continue, liquidly buoyed.
Temperature, not density, determine impact, so clarity's a function of
Breath within air's greatest solidity. Where truth may be a process of reach
And grasp, touch, the byproduct, overwhelms to accentuate contact. Love
Defines substance and potency thus, somnolent so carnal. A system
Of proportions based on blazing and melody makes sense only in an
Explosion's moment. Memories ignite perhaps in its keeping, but actions
Lose all purpose, amplify denatured in a culture of grooming. Where looks
Matter, what's seen has no vision and is subject to power, thus, except
Perception too sparks in detonating.

Any entity based on expanse precludes being, scans the world as image
And machine. There, whatever's benign deactivates and time's promise
Of ending looms shallow. Located, anyone's a patch of faults, packaged,
Bundled up to roll. A fly could spoil your's minute, so. A bird could revive it.
A scent. Movement anchors people in amelioration, a farce, but all they've
Been taught. Since improving requires proof, it's useless. But somebody
Comes trained, making the most of judgment, to see both light and dark
As radiant: sustaining. In this mechanics abundance produces sensation
So all, in living, affirm plethora patriotically. My's hope becomes thus
Consumption, but with harmonies, time-released: triumph's first picture.

If winning's suspended, so's living perhaps. But what good's a concept
Of health to whatever occurs? Except without an inkling of sequence,
You's can't be claimed; don't belong to somebody or a future. Swaying,
Then, we're forever, provided all form surges relinquished. My's place may
Be boundless, but any declaration would limit that. In their own scheme of
Heat, shared broadly, we cook. The illusion of freedom in containment's
Unmitigated contentiousness.

So parcels of light were discovered in force, and symmetry in saying their
Uncertainties, but each accounting narrows. Why should expression expiate
Any sorrow, and is a voice's main violence this? To drown experience. Grief
And fear change words into tales, formulate truth into legislate and lawless.
Responsibility names an iteration, clogged song, clearing each throat but
For what if not release? In rightfully representing them, somebody screens
Me's from contact. Through adhesion thus, I separates, and love presents two
With one saying, perhaps a bringing forth, at least patterned.

iii.X

Somebody may regard anyone as loss, live her thus as an opportunity,
Missed. So each pictures others what they are never, and contact becomes
A row of blown fuses, culpable and mined. As a mental past, projected in
Omission, touch can sink to a blister. Pop. At the fork in somebody's path,
Anyone fizzles out. Recurs. One names me's to legislate me's, corralling. They
Kiss us so we're legitimate, spoken so labeled. I purrs, by law enclosed,
Social, humming in song's one realm, an acquiescence that exults. Facts
Conceive themselves from without to override expression's finite shapes,
But at thinking's expense, since knowledge's reportage.

Where just would mean adequate representation, fit pronouncements,
Legal's impossible. Intended to designate, ruling suspends and vocalizing
Imprisons in harmony's name. What's lyrical, meaning flow, brands its whole
Gamut, from inspiration to process through the product. So anyone's words
Consume me's in the construct of amazement. Fascination supplants musing
With monuments, obsessively tangible, indifferent since objectified, insensate,
Reducing to a burn, spewing burdens where I are responsible at last, bear a
Weight, could make things thus right, exalted in aging, ripe. Ownership's
Perishable, where a root ends; where a stem fences, validated, defensive,
And the cat, full again, contains. What's considered perception's such
A warming, from wear, from habits of attachment. Meanwhile somebody
Hosts another real, closed off, undomesticated, an excellence thus.

Grasped, you's are innocent, absolved, simply captivating, captive thus; a
Point. With excrescencies, comestible, for consumption fit, mortal so bound
To be what's divine. Glazed in a status, polished, I orbits, wall or bones,
Circumlocuted without zeroing in. If there's no agreement without limiting,
Anyone's a pattern, template for dimension, a wave, undisclosed yet
Ciphered. Could movement reconstitute me's as a countdown? Between
Outcome and an idea, they're struck, metallic. Dividing's vitality but we's
Sift, a remains; ruins that noise might reanimate, a fever, pitched. Scratch,
So scarring. Can I's undo, without end but in dripping, as a delivery,
Released into feet, into ankles or a floor?

iii.XI

Truth's an assumption or acceptance, so uncertainty. Truth's rubber,
Of gums and temptations, of lips pulling back, invisible, but questioning,
So gifted, where there's allowance, once permission slips, never legitimate,
The nails and extremities brittle, glistens. Not hearing, no attention,
Without span, disbanding, truth's a pregnancy, gorging, abortive. Truth
Liquidates where moving's solution, but, as energy, in packets, an
Interconnective dullness; tissue, woven. Scaling, a vigor, truth mounts,
Geographic, where somebody's one suit's drifting. Claims we move through
Volition, expected.

Truth's liberty isn't something stolen, but original, where I wades through
Each step, an orientation, so illumined, a body of thought, intimate.
Evidence's believing, though they waver, since for humans there's only this
Presence, stem and petal, red, the one knowing in agreement, or else
There's no contact with facts. A drop insinuates the fabrics to everything,
Closed off so truth can take the world's place, in passage.

At the end of my's rope, harmed from transformation, everywhere damaged,
An orality, mouth, on sucking, then applied, they rings valid thus, where
Days are tunes automatically occurring. Impatience ages me's, childish,
Reliant on time's implicit daring, a cough. Hushed, somebody now plays
An antagonist, responsive and too large for according, so eludes it,
Pondered or put, laid in a flourish; then we're jealous of ourself. Truth's
Interactions are sumptuous thus fleeting; drenched, receptive and
Contagious, iterations. Everyone comes from the burning of helium
But truth's its own impulse, thus rolls the dice, openly, some potential
Impetus, so all incarnation and commitment once a story's selected.

I's are slowness, slightly majestic, personalized or tightening, acquired,
And the valve, bubbled up. Where that unwinds my's cells enlarge but we
List, a fringe or strip, selvage, border, division of a hair or bead, flammable,
Arranged, plough or chop. Somebody careens in likeness or hearing, ships
And inclines where sound lusts; truth's desirous. If so, tone's a litany of
Time, where instants, recorded, may be replayed, but can they relive
Or revive, though each is a sum of passage? Everything that's kindled
Returns, but we're stuck on the rim of burning, ponder so leaden. And
Admit all: the morgue, acts of war, innocence. Performance thus validates
Plot, and urge's an incrimination.

If attraction rearranges or disorders bodies, or discards or disbands them,
Its distinction's dissolute. Ruminative, a digestion, chronicle, itinerant, love
Supposes episodes for its trajectory's sake, thus laden. Thus bogs. Does
Fact surprise impulse? Since no interiors can meet, even outwards, counting
Is given in boundaries, enumerates truth as discretion. If song reconfigure
Law into motive, contingent on others' images at least, by the same token
Rule's a wall, so orbits are posted.

Light's limits are perception's occupation or issue. Every surface with
Breath, such as skin may be a precipice but its boundaries fabricate, so
Anyone can go blanketed, inside, held. On an edgeless end, for example
Flesh, touch records all possible telling, passed through or not, code or
Pulse. If so, appearance invents regiment and science, but in whose eyes,
Since that can't be shared? If vision weren't human, and where there's no
Pronouncing, all accounts bear witness. Noise acts continuous but, in
Keeping with looks, contradicts at some unbordered frontier—a wave
Would express this—so one may end without the other.

iii.XIII

The picture of energy's recycling, and not an indefinite path or vibration.
If a span, one that orbits back on itself, in time, where full means
Enclosure. So dwelling, which prohibits the given of errance, dissipates
Impulse with pretexts. Concentration burns, in part in an effort to track
What's invisible, which, through attention, can be gleaned and controlled,
To an extent. Any direction indicates order, dictates rites of development.
Struggle then glorifies all routine, subverts it only as surfacing can; as a
Fork distinguishes current. Diverting doubles virulence, confirms mirth
To destructiveness, where aversion introduces recurrence; an example's
A dream.

Wary of knowing's mistakes, somebody parcels information to ignorance,
Where mass is comparable, so counts. Housing loss, as each shape does,
They discredits containment; shows holding as dust, an argument. In
Accepting form as imbalance, they might have a grip. Take expression
As proscribed instead, content ourself to drift in that familiarity, choosing
Failure over aberration. In any case irregular, at synchrony's mercy,
Euphoric or not, anyone's drunk, since categories, shutting in or down,
Go to my head as if illumination.

Observing an embrace, in wrapping, lies endlessness, where a fold
Orders. Where wave's an alternance of refusals with denials. Equality is
Measure's imposition: aligns figures with things; generates proportion
By stifling expression, confined. Effusive. So music's method, born from
Adoring, restrict through decoration, and ornament's conduct. In terms
Of objects, imagination's naked; subterranean, a circularity, submerged,
Unpredictable thus. Like memory, flesh can never fully react. Stimuli stun
Them. So skin surrounds and buries, in its own cask even; prefers
Preservation to feeling or grasp, absorbed by impermeability, as a brain
Or any organ, thus.

A wave's all that can be defined, and so beyond describing, abstractly
Active, so energy, a trace. Truth's any surface and its boundless limits,
Radiant, where touching invent, by inversion, interiors, to shelter in this
Or invite somebody. A mirror, water's any intellection; a directive, evident
So proclaimed. Where it dips, light depicts texture, so mimes interpreting,
Mixed. An installation, so lingering, every relation between liquid and
Reflection's a drama, filmed. Skin lays the screen, interval or bound
Between senses and cognizance, an image activated so mechanic, folded;
Dubbed. So between idea and event there's flesh, a delectation, fingers,
With wanting.

A wish can reconfigure itself and others, but only where imagined, so
Visible, articulate regardless of speech, submitted to manipulation. We're
Your doll thus, complicitous, as appearance then, most valid. Habit keeps
One from destroying the other, pent over penchant, and listless.

The function of a wave is its basis in movement, not on the particle
In question. To go on's so loosely defined, a vibration, intuiting at least
Points of attunement, thus pleased. Truth are to surround each thing and
Call it yes. Though about each spot circles a little death, its cushion
Or blanket, cellular. Then a wave, an undetermined connection, coaxing
Moments, shepherds conjunction, mouths, gently explosive. Instances
Detonate to record in forgetting. There's no recall or reach because
Examples aren't human, only perhaps witnessed as such, so still fleeting.

Skin or any surface ignores interiors but puckers; but suggests what could
Be figured depths where anyone adheres, so's gravity. Around each
Occurrence hums its insulation, a precious interment or internment as
Deterrent from time, decorative so possibly a danger, except if it's truth's
Throne, and in owning deposes, thus decomposition. They're this impulse,
So can only succeed in not trying, where force ranks succession without
Access. So what's made's vertical, though flux.

There is delight without happiness even, once I's am foreign to myselves,
Thus appear and appeal. All flesh may be devised for such tenuousness,
A turning or frequency. To circle, so arrive, touch omits but somebody has
Lips, so all's done with porousness; breath even aside. Holes everywhere
Invent air, not the opposite. Each act's a placement in the lake, a plunge,
Where taking hold's one of floating's forms. Seizing's any inhalation. If
Anyone's afraid it is to pause and that there may be no voice, no surface,
Just continuation, no reason unless it's rhyme, a ringing. Hands only feel
Themself through something else: intervals, so internal. But why, to
Reach, must I's forget what I'm scratching?

If heat is what protects somebody from collapse, it's generated not
Without, as love, the blanket, but within, as love is. Your work's just
To support your's warmth, gently, thus an openness; to move in the
Status of inaction, thus trust; to breathe within your's own sights, regardless
Of use. Divided by light, which all energy is, what's not imagination
Diminishes, becomes its own gravity; a braid. Hoarding strength explodes
Me's thus; protects me against my's weight, though pleasure's exodus, and
So opposed to promise; rounds up all selfishness to loss, corralling and
Then gone. Why not claim happiness as identity and if not, what other
Reason for life? Ignoring is aimed, technically, at prolongation, where truth
Backfires. Or, upon location, disbands, short-circuited, an offspring, so
Every joy's our infant.

iii.XVI

If you have a long staircase, someone, a repairman, for example, will rush
Up it fast. If you have a child they can't wait to grow old. Each intent on
Their own expenditure, thus. But joy too orbits in all concentration, any
Personal burning, all dilutions permitted.

Existence is where a baby sees, the moon coming up or a cloud, and says
"Ours." Then on an edge, what persists transmutes through each mouth,
Individual, to a voice, thus singular, so echo. Since ardency encircle,
Anyone, observing the child, becoming outer to their focus, drifts in the
Opened exile of such utterance. Since deliberation's constant this kid
Always is, even if nonexistent, and's revealed through absorption reversed
To centrality, including an abstraction, and, in becoming visible, this
Offspring's separation; appears and at once divides. Then I'm consigned to
My's critical edge, where measure's imbalance. Otherwise, in wishing, in
The five-year-old's whim, things become their intuitions: where senses and
Organs are imagination, activated at last for once.

Because skin's a code, flesh is repetition, ad infinitum, generative; renegade.
Only what's told can't be otherwise expressed, thus excludes sensing.
If a child assume that droplets are peopled; dense bubbled worlds, that's
One truth of any liquid. Seen from inside, a tear's not enclosed, but ends
In expansion, full brimming of sky. So it does. Because an image is
Regardless of mass, any picture's or thought's light escape and radiates.
Distilling crafts its own horizon, full interface, depth; constellates
Illumination to swallow it back, digesting, thus blind, apart from vision.

iii.XVII

Pleasure's independent of expectation, but relies on repeating for conflict,
Its substance. Any singularity's infinite density, imploded. Is imagination's
Use to distill whatever escapes, what it's finally not, to this jewel, perhaps
Nearly invisible? Everywhere a wave's seen, the world ends. To follow's a
Pilgrimage or dream, where there's no logical conclusion, since can what
Are distinct recur?

Since coupling mix codes, somebody's traced. If one fall away, the
Other's point won't coordinate, on a trail of what may be irreparable:
Growth as isolation from truth. If feelings tunneled shortcuts within
Moments, and they may, you's could emerge on another end of now. So
To touch, for example, are out of time, along its peripheries; determination's
Failure, since its second term's unknown. Because definition's based on
Relation, love has no meaning, if unique. At its points of articulation,
Collapses. Beauty's a middle ground then, an easing into absence.

In each moment of joining, that's separation, so fusion and fission the same.
In water, anyone breathes out bubbles which expand the liquid's surfaces,
Incorporate or bloom. If their air contracts, diminish and thus multiplies,
Detonation can spark. Everywhere one entity, such as cells, concentrates,
The chances of exploding abound. If before any occurrence its energy
Gathers, that's an announcement, so everything trumpets into place, in
Passage, but life holds no locus, since we're irrevocably unspecified,
Through confusion breathe. Death too is thus respiration, the other's
Unadulterated vitality, foreign so whole.

If climax is love's physical coherence, then dispersal equals oneness.
Longing is at arm's length, periphery, detachment, so somebody's always
Out of reach, thus a permanence, so with the status of truth; constant.
Somebody's anyone's full extent then, their atmosphere or sky: emotion,
Where luminousness meets itself. Conducted thus, all light's produced,
Not organic; its agency acoustic, odor or attraction. Love comes for
Instance from a temperature change, where crystallize wrinkles symmetry.
Jewelling intervals with the dazzle of faults, love negotiates unwittingly, as
Passage; can circumvent time then: looping. Love's the bargaining, not
The gleam it rents, renders and delivers, in offering up, as to boast
Articulation's not severing.

In adoring, each cancels or refigure another, because they can't touch
What's not. But their only chance is to embrace the impalpable. Each hand
Lies between: mutating and transmission. Then contact's on the verge of
Joining itself, at impression's limit. Ingrown, bulb, exposing time's game.
Circling round to one point blurs and sparks, so ends it. So for waves to go
On, pattern's abandoned. Any shortcut, as in nerves, extinguishes; what
Repeats exhausts. Once a cycle breaks, does rhythm continue, or dislodge?

Logic can't explain water, though wet elucidates thought. A kiss then
Moistens within, and speech glistens. That's talk's use: such internal
Circuitry. Where shapes drip into liquid's a formation, a source, planet
Or braid, tapering. Anyone's relation to invisibilities might be most sensed
In gravity, the shadows of dimensions, as weight propagates, as in only
Mass spreads multiple enough. But why should all shattering break down to
Some indivisible chord? Where duration boomerangs, sound can't tell,
Though the particles at stake may glow; perhaps infinitesimally felt.

The Contemporary Poetry Series

Edited by Paul Zimmer

Dannie Abse, *One-Legged on Ice*

Susan Astor, *Dame*

Gerald Barrax, *An Audience of One*

Tony Connor, *New and Selected Poems*

Franz Douskey, *Rowing Across the Dark*

Lynn Emanuel, *Hotel Fiesta*

John Engels, *Vivaldi in Early Fall*

John Engels, *Weather-Fear: New and Selected Poems, 1958–1982*

Brendan Galvin, *Atlantic Flyway*

Brendan Galvin, *Winter Oysters*

Michael Heffernan, *The Cry of Oliver Hardy*

Michael Heffernan, *To the Wreakers of Havoc*

Conrad Hilberry, *The Moon Seen as a Slice of Pineapple*

X. J. Kennedy, *Cross Ties*

Caroline Knox, *The House Party*

Gary Margolis, *The Day We Still Stand Here*

Michael Pettit, *American Light*

Bin Ramke, *White Monkeys*

J. W. Rivers, *Proud and on My Feet*

Laurie Sheck, *Amaranth*

Myra Sklarew, *The Science of Goodbyes*

Marcia Southwick, *The Night Won't Save Anyone*

Mary Swander, *Succession*

Bruce Weigl, *The Monkey Wars*

Paul Zarzyski, *The Make-Up of Ice*

The Contemporary Poetry Series

Edited by Bin Ramke

Mary Jo Bang, *The Downstream Extremity of the Isle of Swans*

J. T. Barbarese, *New Science*

J. T. Barbarese, *Under the Blue Moon*

Bruce Beasley, *Lord Brain*

Cal Bedient, *The Violence of the Morning*

Stephanie Brown, *Allegory of the Supermarket*

Laynie Browne, *Drawing of a Swan Before Memory*

Oni Buchanan, *What Animal*

Scott Cairns, *Figures for the Ghost*

Scott Cairns, *The Translation of Babel*

Julie Carr, *Mead: An Epithalamion*

Richard Chess, *Tekiah*

Richard Cole, *The Glass Children*

Martha Collins, *A History of a Small Life on a Windy Planet*

Martin Corless-Smith, *Of Piscator*

Christopher Davis, *The Patriot*

Juan Delgado, *Green Web*

Jennifer K. Dick, *Fluorescence*

Wayne Dodd, *Echoes of the Unspoken*

Wayne Dodd, *Sometimes Music Rises*

Stacy Doris, *Knot*

Joseph Duemer, *Customs*

Candice Favilla, *Cups*

Casey Finch, *Harming Others*

Norman Finkelstein, *Restless Messengers*

Dennis Finnell, *Belovèd Beast*

Dennis Finnell, *The Gauguin Answer Sheet*

Karen Fish, *The Cedar Canoe*

Albert Goldbarth, *Heaven and Earth: A Cosmology*

Pamela Gross, *Birds of the Night Sky/Stars of the Field*

Kathleen Halme, *Every Substance Clothed*

Jonathan Holden, *American Gothic*

Paul Hoover, *Viridian*

Tung-Hui Hu, *The Book of Motion*

Austin Hummell, *The Fugitive Kind*

Claudia Keelan, *The Secularist*

Sally Keith, *Dwelling Song*

Maurice Kilwein Guevara, *Postmortem*

Joanna Klink, *They Are Sleeping*

Caroline Knox, *To Newfoundland*

Steve Kronen, *Empirical Evidence*

Patrick Lawler, *A Drowning Man Is Never Tall Enough*

Sydney Lea, *No Sign*

Jeanne Lebow, *The Outlaw James Copeland and the Champion-Belted Empress*

Phillis Levin, *Temples and Fields*

Timothy Liu, *Of Thee I Sing*

Rachel Loden, *Hotel Imperium*

Gary Margolis, *Falling Awake*

Tod Marshall, *Dare Say*

Susan Maxwell, *Passenger*

Joshua McKinney, *Saunter*

Mark McMorris, *The Black Reeds*

Mark McMorris, *The Blaze of the Poui*

Laura Mullen, *After I Was Dead*

Peter O'Leary, *Depth Theology*

Jacqueline Osherow, *Conversations with Survivors*

Jacqueline Osherow, *Looking for Angels in New York*

Tracy Philpot, *Incorrect Distances*

Paisley Rekdal, *A Crash of Rhinos*

Donald Revell, *The Gaza of Winter*

Andy Robbins, *The Very Thought of You*

Martha Ronk, *Desire in L.A.*

Martha Ronk, *Eyetrouble*

Tessa Rumsey, *Assembling the Shepherd*

Peter Sacks, *O Wheel*

Aleda Shirley, *Chinese Architecture*

Pamela Stewart, *The Red Window*

Susan Stewart, *The Hive*

Donna Stonecipher, *The Reservoir*

Terese Svoboda, *All Aberration*

Terese Svoboda, *Mere Mortals*

Sam Truitt, *Vertical Elegies 5: The Section*

Lee Upton, *Approximate Darling*

Lee Upton, *Civilian Histories*

Arthur Vogelsang, *Twentieth Century Women*

Sidney Wade, *Empty Sleeves*

Liz Waldner, *Dark Would (The Missing Person)*

Kerri Webster, *We Do Not Eat Our Hearts Alone*

Marjorie Welish, *Casting Sequences*

Susan Wheeler, *Bag 'o' Diamonds*

C. D. Wright, *String Light*

Katayoon Zandvakili, *Deer Table Legs*

Andrew Zawacki, *By Reason of Breakings*